ORCA
FOOTPRINTS

Wildlife Crossing

GIVING ANIMALS THE RIGHT-OF-WAY

JOAN MARIE GALAT

ORCA BOOK PUBLISHERS

Text copyright © Joan Marie Galat 2024

Published in Canada and the United States in 2024 by Orca Book Publishers.
Also available as an ebook (ISBN 9781459833470, PDF; ISBN 9781459833487, EPUB).
orcabook.com

Library and Archives Canada Cataloguing in Publication
Title: Wildlife crossing : giving animals the right-of-way / Joan Marie Galat.
Names: Galat, Joan Marie, 1963- author.
Series: Orca footprints ; 32.
Description: Series statement: Orca footprints ; 32 | Includes bibliographical references and index.
Identifiers: Canadiana (print) 20230558747 | Canadiana (ebook) 20230558755 |
ISBN 9781459833463 (hardcover) | ISBN 9781459833470 (PDF) | ISBN 9781459833487 (EPUB)
Subjects: LCSH: Animals—Effect of roads on—Juvenile literature. |
LCSH: Wildlife crossings—Juvenile literature. |
LCSH: Roads—Environmental aspects—Juvenile literature. |
LCSH: Automobiles—Environmental aspects—Juvenile literature. |
LCSH: Nature—Effect of human beings on—Juvenile literature. |
LCSH: Wildlife conservation—Juvenile literature. |
LCSH: Environmental protection—Juvenile literature. |
LCGFT: Instructional and educational works.
Classification: LCC QH545.R62 G35 2024 | DDC j577.27/2—dc23

Library of Congress Control Number: 2023946683

Summary: This nonfiction book for middle grade readers explores the science of road ecology and
what happens when highways, wildlife and habitat intersect. Illustrated with photographs throughout.

Orca Book Publishers is committed to reducing the consumption of nonrenewable resources in the
production of our books. We make every effort to use materials that support a sustainable future.

Orca Book Publishers gratefully acknowledges the support for its publishing programs provided
by the following agencies: the Government of Canada, the Canada Council for the Arts and the
Province of British Columbia through the BC Arts Council and the Book Publishing Tax Credit.

Front cover photos by Daniel Chetroni/Getty Images and Jorg Greuel/Getty Images
Back cover photos by lissart/Getty Images, Jasmin Merdan/Getty Images
and mysticenergy/Getty Images
Author photo by Rob Hislop Photography
Design by Dahlia Yuen
Edited by Kirstie Hudson

Printed and bound in South Korea.

27 26 25 24 • 1 2 3 4

For Angus and Jasper, with love

Contents

CHAPTER ONE
LIFE IN THE FAST LANE

CHAPTER TWO
PAVING THE WAY

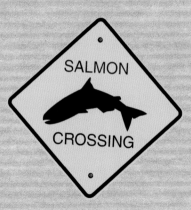

CHAPTER THREE
POLLUTION'S PATH

CHAPTER FOUR
MOVING IN THE RIGHT DIRECTION

Introduction

GPS is convenient when it is available and up to date, but physical maps offer important benefits too. You enjoy greater detail and a better understanding of overall surroundings. Another bonus—you can mark paper maps with your own notes.

My road-trip experiences began well before GPS was invented. Family lore suggests that at age eight, I was not the most patient passenger. Five minutes into a 2,300-mile (3,700-kilometer) trip, I already wanted to know, How many more miles?

My dad was fond of physical maps and always brought a complete collection to guide us. He showed me a trick for finding the answer to my question. All I had to do was locate the tiny numbers between the dots that marked each community along our route and add them up. I remember how the black, red, blue and gray lines tangled across the paper, as if colored threads thrown across the page had been ironed flat. The highways meshing around cities looked chaotic. I learned that every map detail delivers information. Lines—solid, dashed and colored—show whether the track is paved, unpaved, multilane or divided. Brown, green and blue background shades indicate whether

Traveling took my family through regions rich with wildlife. Mom tried to keep my sisters and me entertained by offering a prize to the first one to spot a deer, moose, bear, bison or other animal. I learned to watch for wildlife, like these bison, in roadside habitat. GRANT FAINT/GETTY IMAGES

land is mountainous, heavily vegetated or covered with water. Maps show expressways winding through parks and over rivers. The ones that butt up to oceans can lead to ferry crossings.

What the maps didn't tell me was that roads, so necessary to transportation, are not harmless ribbons of pavement. They are structures that cut through prairie, forest, mountain, wetland and other habitats. Their presence impacts wildlife, reduces **biodiversity** and creates pollution. My road-trip experiences, along with reading news stories about animals risking their lives to cross roads that bisect habitat, made me curious to learn more about how motorways affect the **environment**. I discovered that a relatively new science exists, called road ecology. Experts in this field work to find solutions to the problems caused by the transportation routes we depend upon. As you'll see in the pages ahead, scientists, engineers and other professionals, along with people like you, can help improve habitat and reduce the ways animals are affected by roads.

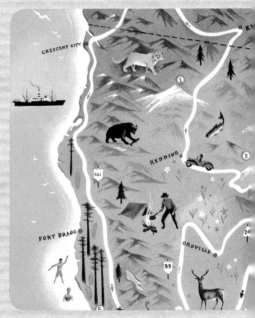

Some maps indicate how land is used or what animal species are found there. They can be used to compare how terrain changes over time, with older maps revealing larger natural areas and fewer roads. Maps can help us understand human impact on the planet.
CSA IMAGES/GETTY IMAGES

CHAPTER ONE

Life in the Fast Lane

SO MANY ROADS!

How often do you need a ride? Highways, streets and avenues make it easier to reach the places you need to go whether you hop on a bike or drive in a car. Roads are a key type of infrastructure that we depend on every single day. They allow you to get to school, workers to reach jobsites and travelers to explore new places. They enable patients to access hospitals and other health services. Roads allow firefighters, paramedics, police and rescue workers to respond to emergencies. Transportation networks also help nations grow their *economies* by making it possible to access natural resources and transport goods between markets. Think about it—have you ever reached a store without using a road?

Roads make it easier to travel between two points. They give freedom. If you could only travel on narrow mud paths, do you think you would go out as often as you do now?
SHARLEEN CHAO/GETTY IMAGES

The more populated and wealthy a country, the higher its road density. Public transportation like buses and light rail transit can help reduce traffic, but people often prefer the convenience that private vehicles offer.
DENNISVDW/GETTY IMAGES

Researchers have tried to determine the number of roads across the planet. Some sources say more than 13 million miles (21 million kilometers) of roadways crisscross landscapes in countries around the world. Others estimate there are 40 million miles (64 million kilometers) of roads on Earth. Either way, that's a lot of map lines! The United States is home to 4.17 million miles (6.71 million kilometers) of roads, and Canada has reported having more than 621,371 miles (1 million kilometers) of public roads. Some are four-lane highways. Others are paved or unpaved lanes that allow two-way traffic. Roads on bridges span bodies of water, and tunnels allow travel through mountains and under water. Road ecologists recognize the important benefits these structures offer as well as the ways their development and use create problems.

Roads like this, built by ancient Romans, allowed soldiers on foot and horseback to travel as fast as 20 miles (32 kilometers) a day. Couriers using horse-changing stations could journey up to 60 miles (97 kilometers) a day.

GERARD PUIGMAL/GETTY IMAGES

ON THE SURFACE

Roads are often paved with *asphalt*, a flexible material created from oil or petroleum. They may also be made of other materials such as soil, gravel, brick, cobblestone or concrete. Engineers estimate traffic levels, noise and costs when choosing materials. They also consider climate. Pavement will soften and expand when temperatures soar. This can stress bridge joints and create ruts and potholes. Roads in the chilly Arctic must be able to withstand the affects of *permafrost*. *Global warming* is causing permafrost to thaw, leading Arctic roads to warp and sag. Flooding, landslides, wildfires and other results of extreme weather caused by climate change also shorten roads' life expectancy. Repairs and construction disrupt wildlife. The presence of people, machinery, noise and light affects animals' ability to use resources in the surrounding habitat.

EARLY ROADS

Roads began as animal paths that humans adapted for their own use. The first constructed roads, however, were built around 4000 BCE. These include stone-paved streets in what is now Iraq, layered rock on the Greek island of Crete and timber roads in England. Ancient Romans became known as the greatest road builders. Some of their thousand-year-old roads are still in use!

They understood that effective transportation routes would bring military and economic benefits and make it easier to manage their territory. They built close to 53,000 miles (85,295 kilometers) of roads, beginning in 312 BCE. The routes connected their capital—Rome—to distant parts of the empire. When possible they were built in straight lines—even when lakes or other barriers were in the way. They set up drainage systems, built foundations and layered rocks and concrete to create roads that were from 3 to 6 feet (0.9 to 1.8 meters) thick. Just as today's construction pushes wildlife out of its habitat, the region's wildlife at that time must surely have scattered to seek new places to live.

But it was unlikely that conservation was a concern. The human population was smaller and wild habitat much greater. Today more than eight billion people live on Earth. Our need to get ourselves, resources and goods from one place to another puts a great amount of pressure on nature.

TRANSPORTATION CHALLENGE

Imagine driving through a forest. Trees stand like sentinels on each side of the road, throwing shade across black pavement. Now picture the landscape during construction. Bulldozers would be used to clear a path through the forest. The tree *canopy*— a habitat where squirrels, porcupines and other species spend much of their lives—would become *fragmented* (broken up). Birds nesting in trees, mountain lions sunning on branches

and moose feeding on **browse** would be forced to make a quick escape. Chicks in twig nests or owlets in hollow trees would not survive the construction. Squirrels hiding cones in **middens** would lose their food stores. Chipmunks would lose access to the soft earth holding their tunnels and chambers. Bats that rely on mature forests to roost and forage, and native pollinating insects, would also suffer from the loss of forest habitat. Even fish would be affected. Tree shade helps keep water temperatures stable. Roots that extend into creeks provide spots for fish to rest and hide. Shade-seeking species would need to find new places to keep cool.

Construction also upsets natural drainage. Workers must try to prevent sediment from entering wetlands, but they are not always successful. Frogs, muskrats, beavers and other species suffer when habitat becomes degraded—not suitable or available to the species that depend on it. A degraded habitat may no longer provide food, water, places to shelter or the required climate. It stresses wildlife by forcing them to change where they feed, breed and raise young. Disturbed landscapes also give **invasive species** places to thrive.

Biodiversity is impacted when beavers are killed on roads. The dams beavers build create wetland habitat used by a wide variety of animals, including frogs, salamanders, turtles, fish, birds, mink, otter, bears, deer, elk and moose.
DEVON OPDENDRIES/GETTY IMAGES

Animal-crossing signs are erected in areas where roads intersect foraging areas, migratory routes and other habitat. Digital signs can be updated with current conditions.
JOAN MARIE GALAT

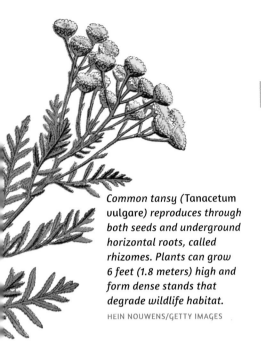

Common tansy (Tanacetum vulgare) reproduces through both seeds and underground horizontal roots, called rhizomes. Plants can grow 6 feet (1.8 meters) high and form dense stands that degrade wildlife habitat.
HEIN NOUWENS/GETTY IMAGES

Plants along roads create buffers that help muffle traffic noise. Roadside vegetation can also provide habitat, but it may reduce visibility and increase the risk of wildlife-vehicle collisions.
MADSCI/GETTY IMAGES

TAKING OVER

Seeds from invasive plants may arrive on construction equipment and mulches used to landscape ditches and **medians**. They often take hold in disturbed soil and spread so much that they replace the native plants wildlife depend on. Common tansy is an invasive species in North America that can produce more than 50,000 seeds a year and interfere with reforestation. These and other plant bullies are a significant biodiversity threat. They can reduce available water, trigger erosion and cause serious road damage. Habitats need a variety of herbs, shrubs and trees to be healthy and support native animal species.

Like invasive plants, nonnative animals can be a problem too. They thrive due to the lack of natural predators in their adopted habitats. Green iguanas are an invasive species in places that include Florida, Texas and Hawaii. Able to grow up to 5 feet (1.5 meters) long, they cause damage by burrowing beneath road

embankments and stabilization walls. Transportation workers feared tunneling green iguanas might cause parts of Florida's Turnpike to collapse. They undertook repairs, but mending roads is only a temporary solution. Invasive plants and animals cost millions of dollars in maintenance and repairs in the United States each year.

Public roads are a government responsibility. Transportation planners must consider how roads will impact the environment. They need to examine the risks of pollution, greenhouse gas emissions and direct loss of habitat. They must also consider indirect habitat loss that occurs when **watersheds** are disrupted and **ecosystems** become fragmented into smaller, isolated patches. Moving soil, rocks and vegetation can upset natural watersheds and create drainage problems and landslide hazards.

Pet owners who find that their green iguanas have grown too big to keep sometimes release them into the wild. This illegal practice worsens invasive-reptile problems. Weighing up to nearly 20 pounds (9 kilograms), green iguanas that cross roads or bask on pavement endanger drivers and their passengers.
ULLIMI/GETTY IMAGES

Black bears use their strong, curved claws to climb up and down trees, as well as structures like this fence along the Trans-Canada Highway. Roads and railways, as well as habitat fragmentation, contribute to reduced bear populations.
©PARKS CANADA/SARAH FASSINA

ROAD TEST

☑ TRUE or FALSE ☒

Fences can stop bears from reaching roads.

If you suspect this is true, you're wrong! In Canada's Banff National Park, black bears climb 8-foot (2.4-meter) fences to reach vegetation, including nutrient-rich dandelions growing in roadside ditches. Wildlife specialists worked with the Parks Canada highway engineering team to create a solar-powered solution. They set up an electric wire that produces a pulse of 6,000 to 9,000 volts of electricity. It's enough to discourage bears from climbing but not enough to injure them. The zap is meant to teach bears that climbing fences is unpleasant and discourage them from trying elsewhere. Discover more about fencing as a solution in chapter 2.

ROAD ECOLOGY

Roads are meant to solve problems, not cause them, but balancing the needs of humans, wildlife and the environment is a challenge. The science of road ecology examines how roads and traffic impact ecosystems, as well as human populations and communities. It aims to find ways to avoid and minimize the negative effects of roads, including wildlife injury and death caused by vehicle collisions. Ecologists examine pollution issues including vehicle emissions, noise, artificial light and the chemicals used to melt snow and ice. They consider contaminants from building materials such as asphalt, which contains substances that harm the environment.

Ecologists examine habitat loss and fragmentation and what happens when road construction creates ecosystem **edges.** These abrupt transitions between two contrasting habitats, such as roadside ditches and woodlands, reduce habitat quality.

Wildlife crossings in Banff National Park are for animals only. Hikers and other human visitors would deter animals from using the crossings.
HOLLY HILDRETH/GETTY IMAGES

They also create small habitats with a climate that differs from the surrounding area, called **microclimates**. Edges can change levels of light, moisture, soil, vegetation and wind, making habitat less useful to certain species but more useful to others. Problems occur when species compete with one another for available resources. When one species is better than another at adjusting to edge conditions, an imbalance occurs, which negatively impacts the diversity of wildlife in an area.

Motorists driving through this tunnel may not realize it protects both people and animals from deadly vehicle-wildlife collisions.
THIANCHAI SITTHIKONGSAK/GETTY IMAGES

ANIMAL SPOTLIGHT: LARGE MAMMALS

Wild animals travel in search of food, water, shelter, mates and nesting sites. They also need to escape predators. Roads and traffic can make movement difficult and dangerous, and animal mortality on roads is a global problem. One death may lead to another as bears, coyotes, ravens or other scavengers visit roads to eat carcasses. When animals are injured and killed, local populations suffer, and **food webs** are upset.

Banff National Park in Alberta is home to the world's longest ongoing wildlife-crossing research program. Black bears, grizzly bears, bighorn sheep, cougars, coyotes, wolves, deer, elk and moose are just some of the species that live here. The park has erected 51 miles (82 kilometers) of fencing to prevent wildlife

It's tempting to stop when you see an animal like this grizzly bear near a road. The best choice, however, is to drive by slowly. Repeated human contact makes animals less afraid of people and more likely to be struck by vehicles or act with aggression.
JOAN MARIE GALAT

15

SAFE PASSAGES

Planners must understand how different species of wildlife behave in order to find ways to keep them off roads. They examine which species live within a habitat, their population sizes and how well they have responded to solutions in other places. They may use GPS trackers to monitor movement and find out where species prefer to cross highways.

Moose that seek the salt used to deice roads may approach stopped vehicles and lick salt from them too. This puts moose at risk of being injured or killed. Moose that explore roads also put people in danger of deadly moose-vehicle collisions.

JOAN MARIE GALAT

from crossing the Trans-Canada Highway, six **overpasses** that allow animals to cross above the highway, and 38 **underpasses** that go beneath the roadway. These important structures reduce **roadkill** and connect key habitats on each side of the highway.

After wildlife crossings are built, animals must learn to use them. It's taken up to five years for grizzly bears, wolves and other wary species to adjust to the infrastructure. Elk have proved braver, with some even crossing during construction. The new connections prevent roadkill and promote **genetic diversity**—a range of traits being passed from parents to offspring within a species or population. Genetic diversity makes it easier for animal populations to produce healthy young and adapt to changes in the environment.

SHIFT GEARS: STEERING CLEAR OF CRITTERS

All aspects of construction—from mining for materials to managing waste—affect the environment. Some countries set laws that require **environmental assessments** before highways and other roads can be built. This process helps figure out how projects might affect habitat. Regulations may allow the public, governments, scientists and **nonprofit groups** to take part. Some ensure Indigenous Peoples in the affected area are invited to provide feedback. An assessment might show that a project will interfere with people's ability to access food sources they rely on. It might show that plant and animal species will decrease or that shorelines will be altered. Reports include **mitigation measures**—actions to reduce, stop or control problems that might occur. They may suggest restoring habitat or paying people affected by harmful effects. Assessments are an important step in working toward environmental protection, but they do not guarantee that the environment will be put ahead of goals to reduce construction costs.

ROAD TRIP: LOOK PAST THE PAVEMENT

One way to help wildlife is by being a backseat driver—a person who offers advice to the person controlling the vehicle. Help protect human safety by scanning roads and ditches for animals, especially at dusk and dawn when many species are more active. Remind drivers to slow down when they see animal-crossing signs or roadside reflectors. These are placed in areas where animals are frequently seen and collision risks are high. Watch places where visibility is limited, such as the top of hills and the start of curves. Pay attention if you see eyes shining in your vehicle's headlights, and if you see a critter, ask the driver to slow down. It may be part of a pair, group or herd, and they may not continue in the direction they appear to be going. Be sure to pay equal attention to both sides of the vehicle. Look beyond areas lit up by vehicle headlights and ask the driver to slow down if oncoming vehicles flash their lights. It might be a warning that animals are on the road. The species you encounter will depend on where you're traveling, the season and time of day. Raccoons, for example, are more active at night.

Passengers can help drivers watch for wildlife by paying extra attention when traveling through or beside habitat. This includes farmland, forests, wetlands, stream crossings, lakeshores and other natural areas.
JASMIN MERDAN/GETTY IMAGES

HIGHWAY PATROL

Around the world, road designers and communities use tricks to encourage drivers to slow down. They might place a curve before a stop sign, install speed bumps or paint art on roads. These strategies may be designed to protect pedestrians and cyclists, but they can also save the lives of pets, domestic species and wildlife if traffic slows down. Signage reminds drivers that they may encounter animals. Wildlife-vehicle collisions can result in human injury and death, cause damage to vehicles and lead to traffic delays. Hitting an animal is an upsetting experience that everyone wants to avoid. Which signs have you seen?

CHAPTER TWO

Paving the Way

Roads are expected to become a bigger problem for animals like this wolf as climate change leads species to seek suitable habitat. Building tunnels to improve connectivity is an important climate-adaptation strategy.
HIGHWAY WILDING

MIMICKING HABITAT

Have you ever stepped into a dark haunted house at an amusement park? It's hard to feel safe when you don't know what surprises might jump out at you. Animals feel the same way. They do not want to enter wildlife crossings that make it hard to tell if danger lies ahead. They need to know passages will not expose them to predators or allow them to become trapped.

The most effective crossing structures mimic animals' natural habitat. They may have grates to add light or be designed to maintain a particular level of moisture. Natural features are created with brush, logs, tree stumps, soil or rocks. Fencing, hedges or walls made of earth or stone can guide animals away from roads and toward crossings. As well as reducing wildlife-vehicle collisions, overpasses keep habitats connected, especially for grizzly bears. Road ecologists, however, may propose tunnels or underpasses for small to medium animals, including mammals, reptiles, amphibians, fish and other aquatic species. Wildlife underpasses are less expensive to build than bridge crossings. They can be built with round or elliptical culverts, usually made of cement or metal. Square-shaped passages, called box culverts, allow larger wildlife to pass under roads. As with overpasses, fencing may be used to direct larger species toward crossings.

ROADKILL

Collisions between vehicles and wildlife are a costly problem. Some animals are attracted to roads. They use them to travel, reach food sources and access salt left by *deicing.*. Tracking roadkill helps scientists collect data they can use to reduce animal deaths and improve road safety for people. They learn where different species live and how they behave. Studies also provide information on population size, animal disease and contaminants in the environment. They reveal the presence of invasive animal species, as well as nocturnal creatures and other hard-to-monitor species.

The Nutty Narrows Bridge, a popular roadside attraction and landmark in Longview, WA, cost $1,000 when it was erected in 1963. Its existence shows what a small group of environment-minded citizens can accomplish.

SAFE PASSAGES

The late Amos Peters noticed squirrels were often killed trying to cross Olympia Way in Longview, Washington. He sketched an above-the-street bridge and brought a team of architects and builders together to help. They built a 60-foot (18-meter) crossing with aluminum and an old fire hose, and named it the Nutty Narrows Bridge. Today the bridge is listed on the US National Register of Historic Places. Eight more squirrel crossings—some replicas of real bridges—have been built in Longview, and locals celebrate squirrels and their bridges at an annual Squirrel Fest.

LONGVIEW, WA. MARCH 19, 1963
NUTTY NARROWS BRIDGE
Constructed by Amos J. Peters, Construction

HIGHWAY PATROL

Bram Koese, a biologist in Amsterdam, was troubled by the number of otter and waterfowl deaths on a country road near the city. He wanted local authorities to respond to the problem and worked with others to bring attention to the issue. In 2021, volunteers set up 642 white crosses along the road to mark the exact spots where vehicles had killed animals. Each cross included the common name of the animal, a drawing of the animal and a QR code linked to the citizen-science platform Observation International, which provided details on the roadkill incident.

overstekende otter

Volunteers helping turtles cross roads are taught to use two hands, never pick up turtles by the tail and always deliver them to the side of the road they are trying to reach. It's important to use clean hands, free of insecticides or lotions, and to wash thoroughly afterward with soap and water.

JOSE LUIS PELAEZ INC/GETTY IMAGES

ROAD MAP: LONG POINT CAUSEWAY

In 2003 the Long Point Causeway, a road less than 3 miles (3.6 kilometers) long, was considered one of the world's worst locations for turtle roadkill. The causeway—part of the Long Point Biosphere Region on the north shore of Lake Erie, Ontario—runs through a **UNESCO biosphere reserve**. The region has the highest wildlife density in Canada, and the **biosphere** is home to more endangered species **per capita** than any other part of the country.

The causeway bisects key habitat, forcing animals to go back and forth across the road to reach food, breed and nest. One hundred species and about 10,000 animals were killed annually before crossings were installed, with frogs, snakes and turtles frequent victims. An improvement project paid for 2.8 miles (4.5 kilometers) of wildlife barrier fencing and seven tunnels, or culverts, to reconnect habitat. The tunnels were placed within 164 yards (150 meters) of one another to stay within the turtles' roaming range.

The project led to an 80 to 90 percent reduction in deaths in the high-traffic stretch where it was installed. At-risk turtles and snakes used the crossings, as well as frogs, mink, weasels and other animals. The culverts have produced an additional benefit—improved water quality and conditions that enable Lake Erie fish to once again spawn in traditional habitats.

ANIMAL SPOTLIGHT: SMALL AND MEDIUM MAMMALS

Road-ecology research tends to focus on large species, but conserving biodiversity means finding ways to protect creatures of all sizes. Small animals play important ecosystem roles, including the spread of seeds and transfer of nutrients to soil. They are food to predators and may also prevent vegetation overgrowth.

Crossings for small animals need their own designs. They must be built in suitable habitat, away from noise and human activity, and include plenty of cover. Crossings also require careful placement. Animals smaller than 11 pounds (5 kilograms) have limited ability to travel great distances. They cannot go far in search of new habitat when roads interrupt their spaces.

In a roadkill survey of small and medium animals—under 66 pounds (30 kilograms)—researchers in Quebec counted 893 carcasses on a 42-mile (68-kilometer) stretch of four-lane highway over four summers ending in 2015. Species found included 47 red foxes, 46 groundhogs, 42 striped skunks, 41 snowshoe hares, two lynx and 366 porcupines.

ROAD TEST
✓ TRUE or FALSE ✗

It is possible to help increase biodiversity.

If you answered true, you are correct! Whether you have a balcony plant, flower bed or garden plot, you can help animals in your community. Grow native species and remove invasive plants. Create natural habitat by piling rocks or tree branches or adding logs or stumps. (Just avoid removing materials from places where they already provide habitat.) You can also make a rain garden by steering water away from roofs, pavement or other hard surfaces that can't absorb water. Direct the water into a bird bath, low hollow on the ground or toward foliage—never toward buildings.

Porcupines are slow-moving animals willing to enter open landscapes and spaces like roads. With more than 30,000 quills each, they are confident that predators will stay away, but this defense does not protect them from vehicles on roads.
JÉRÔME SPAGGIARI/GETTY IMAGES

Slow-moving and nocturnal, porcupines are especially at risk in the spring, when roadside vegetation emerges, and in the fall, when they seek mates. Porcupines give birth to only one porcupette each year, a factor that makes them more vulnerable. In a specific location, collisions can threaten a species' survival.

SHIFT GEARS: PUTTING UP FENCES

As you've seen, fencing may still be used to keep animals off roads. A closer look, however, shows that it's not a perfect solution because it blocks movement. It is used because collisions in certain areas are seen as a bigger threat and fencing, although costly, is less expensive than building tunnels or overpasses. Planners identify migratory patterns and roadkill hot spots—areas where animals tend to be hit. They look at how far target species will travel to get around barricades and how they might respond. Will they tunnel or climb over?

The land's physical nature is considered. Is it flat or mountainous? Is the ground rocky, wooded or swampy? Climate is examined too. Fencing material may expand and contract in extreme temperatures, leading to warps, sags or cracks. Drifting snow could allow animals to step over fences. Planners also look at how nearby land is used or might be used in the future.

If fencing is selected as a solution, the ideal length must be determined. A too-short fence will lead to more crossings at fence ends, while longer structures improve the odds animals will move away from the road or toward a wildlife crossing, if one is available. One study found that fences shorter than three miles (five kilometers) were 53 percent effective in reducing collisions, while longer fences reduced them by more than 80 percent.

Mule deer naturally travel long distances daily and seasonally, but many will reduce their movements to avoid crossing busy highways. Fencing can steer deer toward safe road crossings, but it also fragments habitat and can isolate breeding populations.

AKCHAMCZUK/GETTY IMAGES

ROAD TRIP: NOTE NATURE'S RHYTHMS

Next time you cruise down a highway, watch for wildlife fencing and crossings as well as construction. Experts expect that by 2050 another 16 million miles (25 million kilometers) of paved roads will be built in and through regions rich in diversity. See how many types of habitats you can spot as you look out the window. Depending where you go, you might observe prairie, forest, desert, water bodies, shorelines, foothills, mountains or other natural areas. Look for altered landscapes such as farm fields, pastures, gardens, lawns and artificial aquatic zones including canals, stormwater ponds and irrigated land.

Reduce your impact on the environment with good outdoor habits. If you're walking through a natural area, for example, leave the landscape as you found it. Stay on trails to avoid crushing plants. Never peel bark, break branches, pick flowers or cause other damage. If you lift rocks or logs to look for insects or other creatures, put them back in the same place to protect animal homes. Speak in quiet tones to ensure you do not stress wildlife or interfere with their ability to communicate with one another. Keep your footwear mud-free to avoid spreading seeds from invasive plants between landscapes. Take your trash with you. Consider hauling out other litter too.

Hiking trails allow people to experience and enjoy nature. Like roadbuilding, however, trail construction results in vegetation loss. Land managers can use environmental assessments to help plan, establish and maintain trails in ways that reduce damage to natural areas.

TOM WERNER/GETTY IMAGES

JEFF R CLOW/GETTY IMAGES

ON THE SURFACE

A survey of the world's most deadly roads names a portion of the Trans-Canada Highway between Golden and Revelstoke in British Columbia. This winding, mountainous route, which includes Rogers Pass through Glacier National Park, contains high traffic and plenty of wildlife. Travelers add to traffic problems when they stop to view animals. Bear jams occur when drivers block lanes or park in places that restrict vehicle flow. Some people leave their cars and mill on the road, putting themselves at risk of both bear attack and getting hit by a vehicle. This deadly road is a problem for animals too. Bears that become used to humans are more likely to behave in ways that lead to collisions and human-bear conflicts.

CHAPTER THREE

Pollution's Path

DUST AND DEBRIS

Around the world, most people live, work or attend school near a major road, airport or railroad. These transportation routes expose people and animals to pollutants such as carbon monoxide, nitrogen oxides, benzene and *particulate matter*—solid particles and liquid droplets in the air, including dirt, dust, smoke and soot. If you've caught a whiff of diesel exhaust, you've breathed a type of air pollution that can be found on roads.

Unpaved roads and construction sites are sources of unwanted particulate matter too. The smallest particles can enter a person's lungs. The Environmental Protection Agency (EPA) examined the public-health impact of emissions along major routes, particularly for those who spend a lot of time near major roads. They found asthma, bronchitis and other health issues. Particles also contribute to the formation of *acid rain*, which can make water bodies unsuitable for fish. Acid rain may damage vegetation, as well as paint, buildings and other objects.

Dust and other construction pollution can harm plants and animals directly and also diminish the habitat, food and water that species need to survive.
KATARZYNABIALASIEWICZ/GETTY IMAGES

Passenger vehicles are sizable contributors to air pollution. They emit smog-forming elements such as carbon monoxide and other toxins at road level, where they can enter the food chain and negatively affect the availability and quality of food.
TOA55/GETTY IMAGES

Furthermore, dust from unpaved roads creates dangerous driving conditions when it affects drivers' ability to see. Dust can reduce crop yields and increase road-maintenance costs. Chemicals that absorb water from the air are often applied to roads to help dampen dust, but this solution creates polluted runoff, which can contaminate roadside vegetation and enter local waterways.

ROAD TEST

✓ TRUE or FALSE ✗

It's impossible to reduce air pollution near roads.

If you answered false, you're correct. Methods do exist, including stricter laws on vehicle emissions. Help make a difference by encouraging the drivers in your life to reduce idling—a habit that wastes fuel and pollutes the air. Instead of using drive-through service at fast-food restaurants, park and go inside. If you're one of the millions of kids who ride a school bus, ask your school district to discourage idling. Diesel fumes aren't good for anyone, but children breathe at a faster rate than adults, making them more susceptible to air pollution.

WATER MUST FLOW

Have you ever sprayed someone with a hose? You've probably noticed how water that misses your target soaks into the ground or flows away. Runoff, whether from human or natural sources, journeys over land and hard surfaces like pavement, eventually reaching streams, rivers and oceans. It delivers water to plants and recharges under-the-surface reservoirs called groundwater. When runoff trickles from roads, however, pollutants get mixed in with it. Road-surface pollutants come from deicing salts, herbicides, brake-pad dust, road-construction materials and other sources. They spread into habitat and water used by people and wildlife.

Roads and traffic are believed to be the chief origin of microplastics reaching oceans from land environments. Tire particles are the biggest source, followed by particles from painted lines and other road markings. Some sources estimate that 6.6 million tons (6 million tonnes) of tire rubber enter the environment every year.

Tires are usually made from synthetic rubber—a plastic polymer made from crude oil—along with metal and other compounds. Their particles contain toxic compounds and are harmful to organisms in freshwater and ocean environments. An engineering study found more than 55 tons (50 tonnes) of particles from tires and roads reach local waterways each year in British Columbia's Okanagan region. Simply by driving between lake communities, motorists contaminate local aquatic habitats.

Pollutants in road runoff can kill fish and other aquatic life. Solutions to help prevent pollutants from reaching waterways include filtering runoff through suitable plant life near watercourses and incorporating natural wetlands.

(TOP) 4U4ME/GETTY IMAGES;

(BOTTOM) WIRESTOCK/GETTY IMAGES

ON THE SURFACE

Ice roads are built to create driving routes over frozen water bodies. They connect remote locations and allow oil, gas and mining industries to operate. Canada is home to about 6,214 miles (10,000 kilometers) of ice roads. Creating one mile (1.6 kilometers) takes 1 to 1.5 million gallons (4 to 6 million liters) of water and ice, but removing liquid and ice from a water body can have a negative impact on fish and other aquatic life. Pollution on ice roads from spilled fuel or other hazardous materials is also a risk.

JAMES_GABBERT/GETTY IMAGES

LIGHT AND NOISE

The impacts of pollution extend beyond a road's borders to an area called the ***road-effect zone***. It can stretch hundreds of yards (meters) on each side of a road. Noise and light pollution in this zone create problems we may not think about.

Suppose you need to warn your friend about a menacing dog coming down the street, but the roar of a mammoth truck drowns out your voice each time you try. Birds, frogs and other wildlife near roads also need to be heard. Birds call to warn about threats, engage in courtship and declare their territories. Not all species can change their tunes to overcome noise. Those unable to adjust must find quieter habitat, leaving only noise-tolerant species near roadways.

Streetlights and headlights impact roadside ecosystems adversely too. Nocturnal animals are adapted to living in darkness. Light at night can make it hard for them to seek food and avoid enemies. Species that are active in the day need dark at night to sleep and hide from predators. Some bird species fly toward artificial lights, while others avoid them. Both responses are harmful because the lights upset natural behaviors and cause birds to waste energy they need to seek food, breed and care for young. Light and noise in the road-effect zone can also impact animals' willingness to use wildlife crossings.

The size of the road-effect zone varies for different animal species. Researchers have found the zone is up to 3,281 feet (1,000 meters) for bats and certain bird species, but it extends as far as 3.1 miles (5 kilometers) for some mammals.
DAVID HANSCHE/GETTY IMAGES

SAFE PASSAGES

Watch for tunnels under rural roads next time you are in cattle country. These passages allow cows to graze in pastures on both sides of the roads. Cow tunnels spare farmers the chore of herding livestock and help save on feed costs. Domestic animal crossings keep dung off roads and vehicles, and may stop livestock waste from draining into roadside soil and waterways.

In Waikato, New Zealand, motorists became fed up with livestock poop and smells. The district council responded by encouraging farmers to build underpasses. Farmers were responsible for design and installation and were offered money to help pay for the project.

Roads create gaps in tree canopies, preventing animals like sugar gliders from crossing. Glider poles may be erected on each side of the road and on medians. On average, sugar gliders can glide up to 33-44 yards (30-40 meters).

MEET A ROAD WARRIOR

Alberta's Banff National Park (BNP) is home to more animal crossings than any other place in the world. Much of the wildlife here lives in or moves between mountain valleys, and that's where the first roads in the park were built. Wildlife crossings and fencing were eventually proposed as a safety solution, but many people thought the idea foolish. Some doubted animals would use the passages. Others thought wolves would herd prey toward fences and kill them in sight of tourists.

Parks Canada carried out environmental assessments and chose to move forward with wildlife crossings. Tony Clevenger is a wildlife research scientist who spent 17 years studying the park's crossings. Clevenger and his colleagues monitored animal tracks and later set up motion-activated cameras. They collected hair samples from barbed wire and used ***genetic*** testing to learn how many bears used the crossings and whether the crossings improved genetic diversity by enabling breeding between different population sets.

In the end, the data showed 11 large animal species used wildlife passages more than 150,000 times and that crossings led to 80 to 90 percent fewer large wildlife species being killed over the 17-year study. Clevenger's data and other road-ecology studies helped prove that wildlife crossings are effective. Today nations around the world look to BNP's overpasses and underpasses to help them find ways to connect populations across roads and reduce the amount of wildlife being killed in traffic.

ANIMAL SPOTLIGHT: BIRDS

If an alien asked you to define birds, you would surely point out their most obvious trait. Birds fly! It's easy to think that roads don't stop birds—except for emus, penguins and other outliers—from reaching habitat on each side of a highway. But roads are in fact barriers for certain flying species, including a songbird called the wrentit.

Native to California and Oregon, wrentits have short wingspans that make crossing large highways difficult. A study on genetic diversity on two sides of California's Highway 101 showed wrentit populations were not crossing from habitat in the Santa Monica Mountains to more northern habitats. As it does for other animals, broken-up habitat can make it hard for birds to find mates and maintain genetic diversity. If climate change alters the green spaces wrentits need, and roads stop them from seeking new landscapes, populations will suffer.

California's wrentits are one of the species that will benefit from an $87-million wildlife overpass being constructed over Highway 101. The Wallis Annenberg Wildlife Crossing, which is expected to be complete in 2025, may be the world's largest at 210 feet (64 meters) long and 174 feet (53 meters) wide. You can imagine the size by picturing six school buses lined up behind one another and twenty more side by side. Vegetation on the overpass, including the chaparral and sage scrub wrentits depend upon, will create the continuous habitat they need. The crossing is expected to benefit other birds as well, allowing them to avoid traffic by flying or otherwise making their way across the passage.

A male cougar in Los Angeles, called P-22, was struggling to live in just 8 square miles (13 square kilometers) of land, an area much too small for him. Residents, including Hollywood stars, wanted to help P-22 and other local wildlife access larger habitats. Their donations, along with help from the Annenberg Foundation, resulted in this wildlife-crossing project.

SANTA MONICA MOUNTAINS NATIONAL RECREATION AREA/ WIKIMEDIA COMMONS/PUBLIC DOMAIN

HIGHWAY PATROL

Canada geese often appear on roads, sometimes with flightless goslings trailing behind. Ducks cross too, often while leading ducklings from nest to water. Mallard ducks may make a 1.2- to 1.9-mile (2- to 3-kilometer) journey! Drivers must first think of their own safety and that of other drivers. That means not swerving, stopping or leaving your vehicle and stepping into traffic. The best way for motorists to help is by slowing down when waterfowl is present. Geese that grow used to stopping traffic are more likely to be hit when they move onto busier roads where drivers do not or cannot stop.

LISSART/GETTY IMAGES

SHIFT GEARS: PREVENT SWOOPING

Traffic results in the deaths of millions of birds every year. Barn owls are one of the most at-risk species on major roads in the United States, Canada and Europe. Why? Because they hunt in road-edge habitat. ***Ornithologists*** estimate more than 1,500 barn owls are killed every year along a 154-mile (248-kilometer) section of the Interstate 84 in Idaho. This is among the world's highest highway mortality rates for barn owls.

One of the factors that puts this family at risk is that it seeks prey while flying. Barn owls are nocturnal hunters. They glide only a few feet above open ground, listening for rodents, rabbits and other small animals. This leads them to swoop into the paths of trucks and other vehicles, unaware danger is hurtling toward them. Young barn owls are especially at risk of being hit by vehicles as they fan out to new areas after leaving the nest.

It's not easy to design strategies to protect birds from vehicle collisions. Researchers have found that one way to help protect barn owls is to force them to fly higher than traffic. This can be achieved by planting natural screening, such as trees or tall hedges, along busy roads used by barn owls. Another solution is to allow tall scrub to grow in road-edge habitat, making it unattractive to this bird family.

A barn owl's hearing is aided by its satellite-dish-shaped face, which collects and directs sounds toward its ears. The 46 species of barn owl are found worldwide where winters are mild. In Canada, eastern populations of the species Tyto alba *are endangered, and western populations are threatened.*

(OWL) LANGTON-DAVIESPHOTOGRAPHY/GETTY IMAGES, (HEADLIGHTS) KLYAKSUN/GETTY IMAGES

ROAD TRIP: WILDLIFE SPOTTING SECRETS

Spying wildlife before it enters a roadway can help prevent a collision. Improve your ability to spot animals by looking for changes in nature's patterns. Trees in a forest create up-and-down lines while the backs of species like deer and elk present lines that go from side to side. Animals interrupt tree patterns, making creatures stand out—just a little bit—from the forest background. Learn to scan roadside habitat at different heights too. Foxes and coyotes are lower than moose. Hares and skunks are even closer to the ground. Color provides another clue. Dark grizzlies stand out when they cross snowy landscapes. White Dall sheep stand out on dark rocks or ground.

Scan the sky for gulls, crows, ravens, vultures or other scavengers. If you see them circling near the road, try to see what has caught their interest. Are they looking to feed on a carcass on the road ahead? Likewise, coyotes in the ditch may be feeding off a deer or other roadkill. This is a good place to slow down.

Next time you have a road trip in your future, research what animals you might see and learn about their habits. Pay attention to whether species are active at dusk or dawn, in the day or at night. Understanding typical behaviors will make it easier to spot animals in their natural environment.

Elk can be identified by their beige rump patch and darker neck and legs. They live in herds and in some areas migrate between summer and winter ranges, triggered by greening grasses or falling snow. Herds on roads can bring traffic to a standstill.
KATIE DOBIES/GETTY IMAGES

Most birds are believed to have a poor sense of smell, but turkey vultures are different. They can pick up the odor of carrion from hundreds of feet away. Turkey vultures save government departments millions of dollars by scavenging animals killed on roads.
WIRESTOCK/GETTY IMAGES

31

CHAPTER FOUR

Moving in the Right Direction

Storm drains transport rain, melting snow and anything else that falls through the grate to nearby streams, rivers, wetlands and lakes. Oil, gasoline, antifreeze, litter, pet waste, pesticides, fertilizers and other pollutants from roads and sidewalks enter the environment.

EUGENESERGEEV/GETTY IMAGES

RECONNECTING NATURE

Have you ever walked past a manhole cover and heard rushing water? You may have stepped over a buried *watercourse*. Rivers beneath roads are called ghost rivers. Burying them helps hide the sight and smell of sewage, industrial waste and other pollution. Streets and other types of urban development hide waterways in centers around the world, including New York City, Washington, DC, Los Angeles, Toronto, London and Singapore. In Japan, the Uda and Onden Rivers flow beneath Tokyo's hectic Shibuya Crossing, the world's busiest intersection.

Nearly every river on Earth has been modified. Watercourses have historically been changed to move waste out of cities or to reroute water for industry, agriculture or everyday use. Sewage and drainage systems may be topped with roads, parking lots, buildings and other construction. The goal is often to increase usable

A section of Renfrew Creek in Vancouver, BC, once covered by a parking lot, was daylighted after being buried for 100 years. Creekway Park filters stormwater and creates habitat for butterflies, birds and amphibians.
FCHENG62/WIKIMEDIA COMMONS/CC BY-SA 3.0

land and prevent localized flooding. Natural drainage is affected when paved areas replace soil and vegetation. Unlike riverbanks, concrete structures cannot absorb water. If the rivers had not been buried, they would provide fresh water to communities and allow a diversity of plant and animal life to thrive.

Climate change, which can create high volumes of rain and snow, is leading to increased flooding. Subways, basements and other underground structures may fill with water that can rise above street levels. Some cities are realizing that paved-over watercourses are a problem. The solution, called *daylighting*, involves removing pavement and other obstructions over these underground worlds and restoring them to natural conditions.

The area around Cheonggyecheon Stream was once an eyesore, the water filled with pollution. The city hid it with a road in the 1950s, then an elevated highway in the 1970s. Its restoration, completed in 2005, led to better air quality, cooler temperatures and the return of insects, birds and fish.
HIGHANGLE/GETTY IMAGES

ENGINEERING TO SAVE LIVES

A growing global movement wants to see more ghost rivers uncovered. Daylighting can improve water quality, boost natural water flow and restore aquatic and *riparian habitats*. It may also reduce pollution from stormwater runoff. Economic benefits exist too. Daylighting may reduce the cost of treating waste-water. Peeling away pavement can help prevent flash flooding and make it easier for waterways to withstand the effects of climate change. Investors appreciate real estate with green spaces. They would rather build houses near landscapes with water features than along dreary parking lots. Projects that re-establish natural habitat may also offer parks, walking trails or other outdoor recreation.

Before diving in, planners assess how daylighting will affect the environment and seek ways to reduce any negative impacts such as disturbing soil or sediments that hold pollutants. In Seoul, daylighting a stretch of the Cheonggyecheon Stream, which ran beneath an elevated freeway, was a huge success. It provided an important flood-relief channel, added green space and created a popular tourist attraction.

SAFE PASSAGES

In India, Asian elephants cross train tracks as they move through their territory. Steep, narrow banks along the tracks make it hard for the elephants to escape oncoming trains. North American grizzly bears also use railway tracks as transportation corridors, a practice that can result in injury or death. They may be attracted to the ease of travel that tracks provide or to grain that has spilled from railcars or to opportunities to feed on *ungulates* killed by trains. Around the world, researchers are looking for ways to reduce wildlife collisions. Speed restrictions, warning lights and sounds, and even speakers that emit recordings of barking dogs and deer snorting (a sound deer make to warn of danger) are some of the measures that have been tried.

SOURAV DASGUPTA/SHUTTERSTOCK.COM

SMART HIGHWAYS AND SIGNS

Road planning has traditionally focused on building with speed and efficiency. Construction costs tend to affect decisions more than wildlife and habitat concerns do, even with environmental assessments. Good business, however, must consider *sustainability*. It must aim to ensure that transportation routes do not create pollution. Projects to develop and maintain roads should consider how animal and plant diversity, the climate and Earth's limited natural resources will be affected.

Experts are looking to the future with new roadway technologies. Some of these will benefit the environment. *Smart transportation* uses sensors and other tech to manage traffic and improve road safety. Researchers are exploring smart wireless traffic signs that can send messages to vehicles. This would prevent drivers from missing wildlife-crossing signs, especially in poor light, fog or stormy weather. Intelligent highways are expected to be able to send drivers information on traffic conditions, the presence of wildlife and other factors. By guiding traffic away from accidents and other bottlenecks, smart roads will reduce congestion. This will shorten travel time, thus lowering air pollution from vehicle exhaust. As digital technologies emerge, both drivers and wildlife will benefit.

Smart roads of the future will use artificial intelligence (AI) to send safety information to drivers. The data, which will detail lane position, speed and other factors, can be used to reduce repeat events if a collision does occur.

DOWELL/GETTY IMAGES

HIGHWAY PATROL

Rumble strips—spaced grooves on a road—create a sound to warn motorists when they get too close to a road's edge or approach a risky intersection. In at least 12 countries around the world, strips have been designed to produce a melody as tires roll over the gaps. Musical roads help keep drivers awake and alert, boosting traffic safety. The notes on some musical roads become louder at higher speeds, reminding drivers to slow down. Countries with singing streets include Denmark, Japan, Netherlands, South Korea, Taiwan and the United States.

CITIZEN SCIENCE

Citizen science is when individuals volunteer to help with scientific research. Anyone can take part, and there are plenty of ways to collect information that helps road ecologists. One way to assist is by downloading a roadkill app that allows you to report injured and dead animals on roads. GPS technology notes locations for cleanup crews, and researchers may use collected data to identify collision hot spots and animal migration patterns. Apps can be used to figure out the best locations for fencing, underpasses and overpasses. They can also add to knowledge on animal behavior, species distribution and other trends. In Belgium, one study of app data showed a decline in roadkill incidents. Analysts, however, couldn't tell whether this was because crossings were working or because the populations of certain species prone to being hit by vehicles were shrinking.

In some places travelers may legally keep killed animals for the meat. Roadkill in the United States may not be collected on busy highways, in construction zones or in national parks. Harvesters must first ask authorities for approval, and some roadkill apps allow users to request and get permission to keep animal carcasses. Citizen science helps raise awareness about roadkill problems and reminds drivers to slow down in high-risk areas.

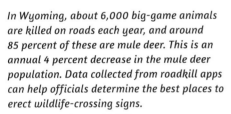

In Wyoming, about 6,000 big-game animals are killed on roads each year, and around 85 percent of these are mule deer. This is an annual 4 percent decrease in the mule deer population. Data collected from roadkill apps can help officials determine the best places to erect wildlife-crossing signs.
CLIFF NIETVELT/GETTY IMAGES;
(INSET) CAVAN IMAGES INC/GETTY IMAGES

ANIMAL SPOTLIGHT: FISH

Have you ever traveled down a highway and noticed that a creek along one side of the road is now visible from the opposite window? It's easy to cross water channels without knowing it. Culverts allow water to flow out of sight beneath roads. They help prevent flooding and erosion but do not always provide the right swimming conditions for fish. Water may be too shallow or have a current that's too swift, or the culvert may even contain a waterfall.

Fish journey as part of their life cycle. They need to access food and shelter, avoid predators, defend territory and reach spawning and rearing grounds. Pacific salmon suffer from barriers to migration. Those that can't reach spawning areas die before they can reproduce.

The Canadian Wildlife Federation reports that roads cross about 170,000 streams with fish habitat in British Columbia. Around 92,000 of these have problematic culverts. At Cross Creek, clogged, collapsing culverts were higher than the stream channel, making it hard for sockeye and kokanee salmon to reach spawning grounds. The culverts were replaced with a soil arch structure to allow fish to travel up the natural streambed. A culvert set on Shuhum Creek also made travel hard for fish. Holes in the rusting metal put them at risk of becoming trapped. In 2021 a new open-bottom arch structure was built to enable fish to reach quality habitat. The rocky bottom on each side of the stream allows amphibians and small mammals safe passage too.

Fish depend on connected waterways and quality habitat to access food, migrate and reproduce. Compare these before and after photos of Shuhum Creek for a clear look at how engineering can be used to create effective fish passages.
(TOP AND BOTTOM) CANADIAN WILDLIFE FEDERATION;
(INSET) MARCUSARM/GETTY IMAGES

Conservation planners must consider warming temperatures, changing precipitation patterns and the frequency of severe weather when building wildlife crossings. As climate change shifts the range of some species, wildlife crossings can help improve animals' ability to travel.

HAGERTY RYAN/PUBLIC DOMAIN; (INSET) JULIA GOMINA/GETTY IMAGES

SHIFT GEARS: BECOME AN EXPERT

Transportation networks make it possible for you to manage your daily life. Whether you're on foot or in a vehicle—or waiting for a delivery—roads are vital to your present and future. They are not going away, and more knowledge is needed to solve the problems they create. Luckily, a great many experts already tackle road-related issues.

Road ecologists look at the big picture. They examine what happens when roads, traffic and the surrounding environment interact. These specialists seek solutions alongside biologists, engineers, landscapers and other experts. Biologists conduct research to understand living organisms in the natural world.

They suggest ways to support conservation and sustainability. Engineers find ways to solve problems with infrastructure. Civil engineers play key roles in designing roads and wildlife crossings. Environmental engineers match scientific knowledge with their ability to design solutions. They take part in activities such as site development, pollution prevention, flooding analysis and site cleanup. Landscape architects use their expertise in restoration, stormwater management and site planning. Community planners help too. They create policies on conservation, transportation and long-term plans. These and other professionals reduce the effects roads have on the environment by using or contributing to environmental assessments. Maybe you'd like one of these careers!

ROAD TRIP: OBSERVE THE EDGE

Roadsides can be managed in ways that benefit wildlife. Pike, walleye, suckers and other fish, for example, will use ditches to migrate. Projects that restore ditches with local vegetation and other features can help fish move between habitats. Next time you are on a road trip, watch for signs of water in ditches, such as cattails, bulrushes and other aquatic plants. Look for ducks, geese or shorebirds, and scan for water-loving insects, including dragonflies or mosquitoes.

Depending on where you travel, you might also spot monarch butterflies and the flowering plant they rely on. Habitat destruction, pesticides and climate change have caused migratory monarch butterflies to become endangered, their numbers shrinking by as much as 72 percent in the last 10 years. Western populations have declined the most—99.9 percent between the 1980s and 2021.

ROAD TEST

✓ TRUE or FALSE ✗

Abandoned roadways are called ghost streets or ghost roads.

If you answered true, you're correct. Decisions are sometimes made to stop maintaining a road, and it falls into disrepair. Neglected roads can turn into crumbling pavement overgrown with vegetation. Roads built for logging or oil and mining exploration can create drainage problems and other perils that put the public and the environment at risk if they are not properly maintained or deactivated—placed in a state that prevents most vehicle use and protects nearby resources. In 2021 a fatal landslide in British Columbia was blamed on unstable land. The Canadian Broadcasting Corporation reported that engineers and hydrologists described the cause as land-management regulations that weren't enforced around old logging roads.

MAREKULIASZ/GETTY IMAGES

Monarch butterflies feed on the nectar of many flower species but only lay eggs on milkweed, the food source that allows larvae to develop into butterflies.

HOLLY HILDRETH/GETTY IMAGES

One way to improve roadside habitat is to remove litter. Animals that eat trash or become entangled in rubbish may be injured or killed. Be safe. Plan to pick with a volunteer team, stay off roads and wear protective gloves.

BJELICAS/GETTY IMAGES

Monarchs depend on one wildflower—milkweed—for egg laying and as a food source during the caterpillar stage, but chemicals used in agriculture have killed both milkweed and butterflies. Researchers experimented with planting milkweed and other flowering plants in roadside habitat and found that roadside conservation might make a difference. More research is needed, however, to learn how best to manage and develop edge habitat for monarchs, as well as fish and other animals.

BE A ROAD ECOLOGIST

Every person can help the environment. Why not begin close to home? Talk with family and friends about the issues you've discovered here and look for solutions in your own community. Could you help reduce roadkill by encouraging drivers to slow down? What if you promoted walking, transit use or carpooling to reduce traffic? How might you improve habitat in your area? Learn about local issues and use your imagination to pave a new way of looking at the dirt, cement and paved roads that criss-cross our planet.

WORD ON THE STREET

People around the world try to protect animals from the effects of roads. You can help too by making sure you never disturb wildlife. Which of the following actions are harmful to animals? Which help?

1.

Walking or using public transit.

2.

Honking the horn while driving through wildlife habitat.

3.

Picking flowers in roadside ditches.

4.

Taking part in roadside cleanups.

5.

Stacking rocks or removing them from natural habitat.

6.

Learning ways to assist in places where snakes, turtles and frogs cross roads.

7.

Feeding deer, bears and other wild animals.

8.

Becoming a citizen scientist.

If you answered harmful for 2, 3, 5 and 7 and helpful to 1, 4, 6 and 8, you are on your way to becoming a junior road ecologist!

Acknowledgments

Firstly, thanks to my parents for the annual road trips. Exploring new landscapes nurtured the curiosity I would need as a future author. Though I wanted to reach our destinations sooner, I now see those hours staring out car windows offered benefits too. They provided space to daydream and form the habit of observing our world, and time to consider how human activity impacts the environment.

Connecting directly with experts on a subject always leads to a richer manuscript. I'm thankful for the kind and generous assistance provided by wildlife expert Tony Clevenger and by Dee Patriquin, P.Biol., R.P. Biol., PhD., a scientist whose research and work have focused on sustainable development. My gratitude extends to Kirstie Hudson, Orca editor, for her astute and insightful feedback, Orca's Georgia Bradburne for her photo expertise, and copyeditor Vivian Sinclair for her attentive review. Thanks to Orca Book Publishers for releasing titles that highlight important topics and to Stacey Kondla of The Rights Factory for her enthusiasm for this project and for her devotion to bringing my work to new readers. A special thank-you to my family for their ongoing support and to Grant Wiens for creating a home atmosphere that enables me to devote time to the themes I want to explore and share.

Resources

Print

Collard, Sneed B., III. CMS 6.43. *Border Crossings*. Charlesbridge, 2023.

Montgomery, Heather. *Something Rotten: A Fresh Look at Roadkill*. Bloomsbury Children's Books, 2018.

Rae, Rowena. *Salmon: Swimming for Survival*. Orca Book Publishers, 2022.

Rae, Rowena. *Upstream, Downstream: Exploring Watershed Connections*. Orca Book Publishers, 2021.

Singer, Marilyn. *Wild in the Streets: 20 Poems of City Animals*. words & pictures, 2019.

Steen, David A. *Rewilding: Bringing Wildlife Back Where It Belongs*. Neon Squid, 2022.

Tate, Nikki. *If a Tree Falls: The Global Impact of Deforestation*. Orca Book Publishers, 2020.

Wilcox, Merrie-Ellen. *Nature Out of Balance: How Invasive Species Are Changing the Planet*. Orca Book Publishers, 2021.

Online

Earth rangers: earthrangers.com/EN/CA/eco-activities

Eek! Environmental Education for Kids: eekwi.org/alien-invaders

Journey North: journeynorth.org

Kids for Saving Earth: kidsforsavingearth.org

Project Noah: projectnoah.org

Project Squirrel: projectsquirrel.org/index.shtml

Scistarter: scistarter.org

Apps

Faunawatch Citizen Science

Map of Life

MISIN: Report Invasive Species

Observation International

RoadkillAPP

Zooniverse

Glossary

acid rain—precipitation that contains harmful chemicals resulting in increased acidity due to pollutants or other environmental factors

asphalt—a flexible material created from oil or petroleum

biodiversity—the variety of different plant and animal species in an environment

biosphere—the habitat in which life exists, extending from below the ocean's surface to a few miles into the atmosphere

browse—the tender shoots, twigs and leaves that some animals eat

canopy—the upper layer of a forest, formed by tree crowns

daylighting—removing pavement and other obstructions placed over underground watercourses and restoring them to natural conditions

deicing—keeping free or getting rid of ice

economies—systems that connect money, trade and the production and use of goods in countries or regions

ecosystems—communities in the environment in which organisms interact with one another

edges—abrupt transitions between two contrasting habitats, such as roadside ditches and woodlands

environment—the place where humans, animals and plants live, including air, land and water; the natural world and the conditions that affect it

environmental assessments—formal processes to determine how a proposed project will affect the environment in the project area

food webs—food chains in an ecosystem that overlap with one another

fragmented—separated into different parts. Habitat that is broken into smaller, isolated patches is called fragmented habitat.

genetic—relating to genes inside cells, which carry information about inherited characteristics

genetic diversity—the presence of a variety of different inherited traits among individuals of the same species

global warming—an increase in our planet's temperature, which contributes to long-lasting changes in Earth's weather and climate patterns

invasive species—organisms that are not native to the region where they are found and are able to live and spread easily, usually causing harm to native species and their ecosystems

medians—strips of land that help stop vehicles from crossing into oncoming traffic

microclimates—climatic conditions in relatively small areas that differ from the surrounding areas

middens—piles of cones, cone scales and other natural debris where squirrels or other rodent species store food

mitigation measures—actions to reduce or eliminate impacts to the environment and its wildlife

nonprofit groups—organizations, such as charities, that operate to support causes rather than earn money for members or employees

ornithologists—scientists who study birds

overpasses—in the context of this book, crossings above roads that allow animals to get from one side of the road to the other

particulate matter—solid particles and liquid droplets in the air, including dirt, dust, smoke and soot; also called particle pollution

per capita—per person; an amount for each person when considering all the members of a population

permafrost—layer of sediment, soil and rock that remains frozen year-round

riparian habitats—land along the edge of natural watercourses, including streambanks and lakeshore. Riparian habitats are transition zones between land and water systems.

road-effect zone—the natural area around a road that is impacted by road surface, traffic and other factors

roadkill—the carcass of an animal killed by a motor vehicle and found on a road

smart transportation—systems that use sensors, automation, communication and other technologies to improve traffic movement

sustainability—relating to the practice of using methods to harvest resources that do not use up or permanently damage Earth's resources

underpasses—in the context of this book, tunnels or

culverts set up to enable animals to travel beneath roadways

UNESCO biosphere reserve—a place that promotes solutions relating to biodiversity and sustainability, designated by the United Nations Educational, Scientific and Cultural Organization (UNESCO)

ungulates—mammals that have hooves

watersheds—land areas that channel rainfall and melted snow through drainage areas to a body of water

watercourse—natural or artificial channel where water flows

Index

JOAN MARIE GALAT is an award-winning author of more than 25 titles that explore nature, ecology, astronomy, engineering, activism and other topics. Her books have won and been nominated for numerous awards, including the Crystal Kite, Skipping Stones, Green Prize for Sustainable Literature, Green Earth, Rocky Mountain, Red Cedar and Hackmatack, among others. A frequent presenter, Joan has traveled across Canada and internationally to promote literacy and deliver science-themed talks. She lives near Edmonton.